Finding Calm in the Chaos

By Leslie Ford

FriesenPress

Suite 300 - 990 Fort St
Victoria, BC, V8V 3K2
Canada

www.friesenpress.com

Copyright © 2019 by Leslie Ford
First Edition — 2019

Edited by Sarah Essak and Jill Courneyea

All rights reserved.

No part of this publication may be reproduced in any form, or by any means, electronic or mechanical, including photocopying, recording, or any information browsing, storage, or retrieval system, without permission in writing from FriesenPress.

ISBN
978-1-5255-5634-0 (Hardcover)
978-1-5255-5635-7 (Paperback)
978-1-5255-5636-4 (eBook)

1. Family & Relationships, Parenting

Distributed to the trade by The Ingram Book Company

Finding Calm in the Chaos

DEDICATION:

I dedicate this book to my entire family.

To my husband: My love for you is enormous, my gratitude is forever.

You stand beside me everyday. You support everything. Forever is a plan that we made in our teens and a plan that we will continue to foster until our death.

The journey has been amazing. We were young, we tried our best, we did our best. We are so proud of our children. We are proud of the friends they have made, and the spouses they have chosen. We look forward too many more years all together.

To Mathew Kierra Kurt and Mitch: You make me proud everyday. You are incredible people. I loved each of you with everything I had, and I continue to do that.

To Stephanie Brad Kaitlyn and Emma: You make me proud everyday. We love having you in our lives. We admire the relationships that you have created with our children. We hope to never be "too much," and we will respect and cherish you everyday.

Mom: You are an incredible lady. I love you, I admire you, I am proud of you and I aspire to be like you. Thank you for loving all of us as you did.

To my Mother In Law: I love you. You are strong and I am grateful for our Mother/Daughter-in-law relationship, it is a gift.

To my mother and mother-in-law together(aka The Ladies): Seeing the friendship between you two is amazing. It is a gift that not many people get to experience. There is a security in your friendship for us and for our children. You exemplify grace and dignity. You taught us many things. We are forever grateful for both of you.

To my siblings and their spouses: I appreciate our similarities, and I appreciate our differences. No matter what might be happening on any given day, there is comfort in knowing that we always have each other's backs. We have a sign in our home that reads "This family is just one tent away from being a full blown circus." This describes us perfectly. What we have is amazing; it is beautiful and rare. I love you all.

And finally to our friends: We love you everyday. Your constant encouragement is uplifting and a great comfort. We value every friendship we have made along the way.

PROLOGUE:

It is a crazy life and a good life. It is a busy life and a forever changing life. We were young parents and now find ourselves young grandparents. Where has the time gone?

As we reflect on our parenting journey we have many memories. As our children go through stages in their lives, we are triggered by their situations and remember similar times for us, but we were younger at those same stages. Does that make things easier or harder? Things were different for us, like they are different for our children. Trends are changing, and the world is a different place. Regardless of the era in which you were born, parenting is a tough and amazing journey.

On our journey, we learned many things, as I'm sure you did on yours. Some good and some maybe not so good. We worked to find our own way. When we look back, we realize the challenges that we faced and the necessity of charting our own course.

We look at this generation and think about the many differences for them, and we try to embrace those differences with the hope of giving our children the support they want and need. We look at the previous generation and reflect on the many differences for them, and we try to understand what life must have been like for our parents. We also try to secure in our minds the things that the previous generation share with us because it is now part of our history and our grandchildren's history.

Parenting trends are changing for the good. According to the information posted on the Stats Canada website families are having fewer children, and in most cases, where there are two parents in the home, the children are being raised with both parents working. A full-time at-home parent is more rare than it used to be. Technology is more prevalent than ever and has presented many advantages and challenges for today's families.

Enclosed are the stories and strategies of our parenting life. My hope is that this sharing will give you some encouragement and new energy regardless of where you are in your own journey.

Leslie

CHAPTER #1

How it all started.

"I have loved that man since I was 10 years old." A statement my mom made when my father was in hospital awaiting surgery after an aneurysm rupture.

My mom's two best friends when she was in Grade 5 remain her best friends to this day. These two best friends are my dad's first cousins.

When my mom was little, her friends would take her with them when they went to the lake for a small weekend vacation, and on route they would stop at their cousins' home to get fresh water. That was my dad's home, and it was where my mom first met my dad.

They were married for 50 years and had nine children. I am the middle child; as in smack dab in the middle: four older siblings and four younger siblings. As my mom would say, "born between two sickly boys."

From an early age, I was independent, always wanting to do my own thing, charting my own course. I always played with dolls and played house and wanted to help take care of my younger siblings. When I was 10 years old, my mom brought home my youngest sibling. I was efficient enough as a 10-year-old to help with bathing her, and I was often allowed to take her in the carriage for walks; I was fully trusted. I just knew how to care for her. With a family the size of ours, it was normal for older siblings to care for the younger ones. I was interested in caring for my infant sister, and with some guidance I proved that I was capable as well. I believe this is where my desire to parent started.

In a house with eight siblings and 11 people at the dinner table, it was necessary to help... and if you didn't offer to help, you were given a job anyway. We didn't have designated chores; we were asked to do certain things when they needed to be done and we did them. In my memory, the girls did way more chores than the boys. My father felt that it was necessary to keep the boys in sports because that would keep them out of trouble and that it was the girls' jobs to help at home! I know... old school.

As we were growing up, we all had different interests and different friends, but the one thing that was consistent and predictable was our home environment. We knew the expectations, and we knew the rules, and we knew the consequences. I didn't like to get in trouble, and so I didn't seem to venture too far away from my parents' expectations. Doing as we were asked and not talking back or challenging my parents seemed easier for me. I watched my older brother struggle to meet those expectations and suffer the consequences. Sometimes those consequences were a loss of privileges or a brief alienation from the rest of the family. My older brother seemed to often challenge my parents, especially our mother. He argued about everything and often had to suffer the consequences. He is an entirely different book.

We all have different memories and yet our collective memories of our childhood are good. We know we were loved, we had clothes and good food. We knew our parents wanted what was best for us, we knew the value of family, and we were raised with the same morals and values. Our home was CALM, but there was lots of chaos.

Mealtimes were busy.

There were times when there were many laughs. There were times when one of us was in trouble and we all got to hear the same lecture. My dad always sat at the head of the table, and when he was finished his dinner he would get himself a cup of tea and some dessert (we always had dessert of some kind). Once he sat back down, he would assign one of us to get our mother some dessert and a cup of tea. On one occasion, when we were all getting older and a few had left the nest, my younger sister, who was bolder than the rest of us, did something unexpected. She was the assigned one to get our mother her tea and dessert after our dad had sat down from getting his own. She responded to his assignment with a question: "Do you have a piano tied to your leg?" The question was followed by a brief silence and then a burst of laughter. To this day, we use that saying often.

On another occasion, my younger brother decided to tell a joke at the supper table. It was a clean joke until the punch line, which involved using the "F" word. We were all in shock. It was funny and scary all at the same time, and it is a moment that is carved in all our memories. He was not disciplined for that moment, but simply reminded of the expectations and warned that using that word would never be acceptable in our home. The kids left the table and laughed hysterically downstairs, but we all knew that he took a huge chance.

My parents didn't have much, but in the spring of 1966, they bought a house in a brand-new subdivision in our small Ontario town. At that time, the bank required a purchaser to have a minimum of $300 in a savings account to qualify for a mortgage. The builder put that money into my parents account so they could make the purchase and then withdrew it again once they got their mortgage. At that time there were seven kids. The house they bought became the home we remember the most. They had that house from 1966 to 2005. It is our family homestead. There were four bedrooms, one-and-a-half baths, and an unfinished basement. Over the years, they eventually had enough money to furnish the dining room and finish the basement, but for many years the dining room was the homework space or the laundry sorting space. My youngest brother came along in 1968 and my youngest sister followed shortly after in 1971. We were three to a room: the three older girls, me with my two younger sisters, and my three brothers. My parents had the master.

Those were chaotic times: We would all go to bed at the same time, which often resulted in goofing around. Some of us slept two to a bed. There was only one bathroom upstairs, and the downstairs bathroom was just a powder room off the back door... How did we manage?

During the winter months, we had a rink in our backyard. My dad would spend hours flooding it for us. He put time into that rink because he knew it was going to keep us busy, tired, and home. We all learned to skate at a young age and love to skate to this day. The boys often hogged the rink for hockey, but usually once a day my mom would designate some time for "no hockey." We learned to skate to the side of the game or within it. We were encouraged to get up early, have breakfast, and skate in the morning before we had to leave to catch the bus because there was no hockey on the rink at that time. The boys were not usually able to get up and be organized to skate before the bus, so we girls could get in a good skate.

The neighbourhood kids have fond memories of the rink as well. It was open to all and used by all. At one time, there were 100 kids on our cul-de-sac and surrounding streets. Some went to different schools, some were younger, some older, but the rink is a fond memory for many of the kids on the street we grew up on.

We didn't travel to see our extended family as much in the winter as we did in the summer because it was a bit of a chore to travel with nine children. In our early days, there were no seat belts, so we were crammed in well. My dad didn't love to drive on his time off because at that time he drove an oil tanker for a living, but we also believe he didn't like the idea of having all of us squished into the car. We remember those times that we did go fondly, but our best memories of travelling were in the summer when we went to the cottage.

My mom's best friends rented cottages at the same time as my parents, so a community of cousins was created each summer at the same place for the same two weeks. We loved going to the cottage. It was not a cottage like cottages you might see these days. It would be more accurate to call them shacks. They were rustic to say the least: very bare, with old furniture and musty beds, but they were all on the lake. The lake is small and just northwest of Kingston, Ontario. Our mom loved the cottage enough to pack up nine kids, all the bedding, all the dishes and cutlery, clothes, and whatever else she needed to make sure we could have this holiday. It was the only holiday my parents could afford, and it was $50 a week. It was as much fun for my parents as it was for us because they could be with their friends and cousins as well. It was a simpler time. It was a wonderful time. It is a traditional holiday that helped to form all of us in some way. It was chaos. It took my dad three trips at the beginning and end of the two weeks just to get us all down there with all the stuff we needed. We had a gigantic orange cooler... I can't even imagine bringing that much food!

My dad's family homestead, where he grew up, was two kilometres from the lake. He didn't love the lake as much as we all did, or as much as Mom did, but he loved that we loved it.

Cottage rule #1: Do not eat at anyone else's cottage.

Everyone struggled in those days. Every cottage had five or more kids. Every family brought just enough to feed their own family. We were free to play and roam, but for the most part we obeyed rule number one.

Cottage rule #2: You may not swim unless someone is watching you.

We gathered in similar age groups. We all had our own group of cousins. We always had our bathing suit on with a T-shirt on top unless it was Sunday when we were dressed for church. But we followed the swim rule until we were teenagers, and at that time we would row over to the island to swim and do our own thing.

Cottage rule #3: Leave the parents alone in the evening.

We used to be able to go out and play in the dark if we didn't go near the water. This is when I remember seeing my mom at her happiest. She loved being with her friends, and she must have loved having some adult interactions, something that was minimal for her back home. We heard lots of laughter and fun when the adults were together. They played a bit of cards, but most of the time they just caught up and reminisced about old times. They just loved to be together. This is where we learned our love of family and cousins; we watched it firsthand.

These were different times. There was no social media, and my mom will tell you that there wasn't an abundance of information about everything like there is now. There were no standards for breastfeeding, or parenting, or relationships. The terminologies were different for dating. If anyone did find out they were pregnant before they were married, it was not talked about ever. In my parents' time, children went to work at a very young age as it was necessary to help provide for such large families. Children didn't question or challenge their parents. There were very few homes where both parents worked. Sunday was a day of worship, and stores closed on Saturdays by mealtime. Very few places were opened on Sunday as Sunday was a day for the Lord and for family. There was a hierarchy of professionals, and doctors were at the top of the list. The woman's place was at home, and the father's job was to provide for his family.

As you read on, there will be stories of how things have changed and how things have sometimes stayed the same. Information is at our fingertips, social media is like a lifeline for this generation of children, and in most families both parents are working full time. Young people aren't getting married until they are in their late 20's or early 30's. Fathers are taking paternity leaves. Religion is not what sets the rules anymore, our youth are challenging their parents and their decisions, and our youth are more independent at an earlier age. It is a very different world now. It is a beautiful world—a faster world—and I believe that now children are smarter and more advanced at an earlier age.

CHAPTER #2

What was it like?

So many words can be used to answer the question "What was it like?"

It was fun.

We never lacked for someone to play with, some place to go, or something to do. My mom had a mantra: "If you don't find something to do, I will find you something to do." Saying we were bored was something we learned not to do at a very young age. We hung out together a lot, and we shared friendships because we were all approximately two years apart, except for the two youngest who were four years apart.

We attended the same schools. We went to church every Sunday without fail. We ate every meal together. Our friends often wanted to come for dinner, and most of the time my mom welcomed our friends to join us. She loved her own friends so much that she wanted us to have those kinds of relationships, but it was the parents of our friends who often said no. Our friends' parents felt like our mother had enough kids to feed.

As teenagers, we ended up on the front step at the same time, all trying to make it in the door before curfew; it was fun.

Our family gatherings were fun. We have great memories in our home, and we have great memories at the lake. The older we got it seems the more we gathered together. Bringing all our kids together was chaotic but fun. We worked hard to build a bond of cousins for our kids like the one we had with our cousins. We gather a lot, and we have lots of laughs. We play silly games, and we are all competitive, which adds to the fun and chaos. With nine kids, and just as many in-laws, 21 grandchildren, and 13 great-grandchildren, most of our times are fun. Our parents did a good job.

It was busy.

Everything we did and everywhere we went had to be well coordinated. Having four kids of my own, getting ready to do something or go anywhere was probably the times when I thought of my mother the most. I wondered how she did it. How do you get nine kids ready to go anywhere, looking the way you want them to look? Packing food, packing clothes, and then organizing the car seems impossible. I remember five of us being shipped to my aunt's house when my paternal grandmother died in 1969. The older three siblings went to the wake and funeral with Mom and Dad. My aunt had eight kids of her own... now that's busy. Planning it, managing it, coordinating it, and trusting it would occupy so much space in my head that I would be late for the wake and funeral if I was able to get there at all.

Imagine baths, sicknesses, getting everyone out the door for school, or receiving everyone after school and emptying school bags, putting away winter boots and coats, doing laundry, it just goes on and on... It was busy, but I would say it was a good busy. I learned that it is okay to be busy and I learned that it is an art to be able to manage busy well.

It was chaotic.

Of course it was chaotic, but if I reflect on my childhood, I don't remember that chaos. Maybe it was more like organized confusion. My mom was practical, and CALM and our family didn't have much. She tells us all now that we worry too much, our kids have too many clothes, we bring too many toys, etc. We didn't have a lot, so she didn't pack a lot.

The chaos is more memorable on the few occasions when my parents went out for an evening to see their family and friends. This kind of chaos was about us younger siblings making it difficult for our older sisters who didn't want to babysit. We thought they were mean. We ran in and out of the house, we refused to eat or acted up at the table, and we did not listen to them. As a result, they were not good babysitters. On one occasion, I remember my older sister being so mad at all of us that she decided she would keep us awake and at the kitchen table to greet Mom and Dad when they got home so we would get into big trouble. When Mom and Dad did finally arrive, we were sent to bed quietly and the next day Mom told us she was unhappy that we didn't behave. No big trouble. I believe that in that moment, Mom stayed CALM, didn't make a big deal of it, but the next time they went out for an evening, she set things up a bit differently so that it wasn't so much work for my older sister. She gave each of us some responsibility, and she explained different expectations for each of us with the understanding that if things weren't going well then, my older sister would have the right to step in. I learned that every situation doesn't require discipline, and a parental reaction can set the stage for CALM or CHAOS.

It was happy.

It was a happy home. We don't have memories of doing without. We don't have memories of being separated from each other. We don't have memories of being cold or hungry. My mom talks about us getting older and realizing that other kids had more and how she was sad when we came to that realization because they couldn't give us more. While this made mom sad, we don't have very many memories of envy.

Our mealtimes were fun, and the food was always good. Our parents didn't fuss over food. We had what we had. My mom didn't make us eat things we said we didn't like because she could never put food to her own mouth if she didn't like the smell. Every meal had dessert, and part of that was making sure we were full. The only seating space that was designated was Mom at one end of the table and Dad at the other. Sometimes the boys were separated, but mostly we sat where there was a chair.

Our home was happy because it was predictable, there was a structure, we were all held to the same standards, and there was a CALM. We knew Mom would be there when we got home from school. We knew the consequences, both good and bad, when we did well or didn't. Our Mom was not a shouter. She was firm, and we always knew where we stood. There was a security in knowing those boundaries. Dad was a bit of a shouter, but I feel like he only shouted when he had had enough, and I feel that those times he shouted were warranted.

Our home was happy because we had traditions. Church on Sunday was always followed by bacon and eggs. Sunday dinners were always at home, even when we all started working. In those days, stores were closed on Sundays, and everyone came home for dinner on Sunday.

It was a happy home. I learned the value of traditions and the value predictability in the home.

It was stressful.

It was a stressful home, especially if you were in trouble. The thing with a big family is that when someone is in trouble everyone seems to get a bit of the discipline. The other thing is that when you found yourself in trouble there was usually an audience.

Doing homework when others where clowning around and dishes were being done was stressful. Homework was done at the kitchen table. There were no desks and no place in our rooms for a desk. Having three older sisters who did well in school was stressful; I always felt I had to live up to that. Having an older brother who hated the fact that I was now at his high school and could see what he was up to was stressful. I was trying to find my way, and he didn't want me around anywhere, which was stressful.

Bringing a friend home was stressful. There was a history of jokes being played, and we never knew what our siblings might do. The man I am married to now is a trooper. He has one brother who is 10 years older than him. Bringing him to our house was stressful for me. He came from a different high school, he was quiet, and my parents knew his parents.

The first night he picked me up at the house, my younger sister stood in the front door crying because she didn't want me to leave. My boyfriend could not handle that. We pulled back into the driveway, and we took her to the store, got her a treat, and then took her back home. When we were pulling away for the second time, my younger brother came running to the door.

I coached my boyfriend to continue, pay no attention, but he couldn't just leave when my brother was working so hard to get our attention. When my boyfriend rolled down the window, my brother shouted to him, "Bring her home on time; it's her turn to have a bath tonight." I wanted to die. My mother says, "It must have been love because he kept coming back." I learned that stress happens at all ages.

It was crowded.

It must have been crowded, but I don't remember feeling like it was that crowded. Our bedrooms must have been crowded, but that doesn't stand out in my memory. We didn't have much, and our rooms were for sleeping. We had a bed and a dresser. Our rooms weren't full of toys or other things.

Going somewhere in the car, certainly we were crowded, I remember that, but we were so excited to go anywhere that we didn't complain.

In 1987, my parents bought a piece of property on a lake. They started to build a cottage of their own. At that time, they had 10 grandchildren, and they could see that this family was only getting bigger. They built the cottage with minimal architectural plans and built it with this ever-growing family in mind. At times, the cottage would have 30 people sleeping in it. The loft was a wide-open second floor with beds, bunk beds, and even a crib. It was crowded. In the summer months, it was anyone's guess who might be there. We always had to be prepared for a crowd and plan accordingly. There were only two bedrooms, and one was for Mom and Dad. The other bedroom was small and was usually designated for the smallest child and one parent. The rest of the beds doubled as couches in the main living area. You were never sure who you would sleep beside on a mattress on the floor. You were never sure who would be the first one awake or what time that would be. You were never sure how many were staying all weekend or if some were just day visitors.

It was a central meeting place. It was a sacred place to all of us. We didn't complain. We accepted the crowd and the environment that went with that. Some managed better than others, but we all loved the cottage, and we all loved our home. I learned that crowds in this family are inevitable. I learned that not everyone manages the crowd the same way, and I learned to respect our different coping capabilities.

It was warm.

Our home was always warm. Growing up in a large family who didn't have much, cold is not a descriptor I would ever use.

Mom hated being cold. Our home always had a warm temperature, and for the most part was warm emotionally as well. However, at times it didn't feel that way. At times, I think each of us took a turn feeling like we didn't belong, or like we didn't like our home, or like we couldn't wait to "get out." We all have some level of anxiety, some of us more than others, but that speaks to our different personalities, parents tiring as time went on, older siblings leaving the house, and just natural changes in our family life.

I remember the death of a young cousin. He had been very sick. He was the same age as one of my younger brothers. We all went to the wake, and we were all very sad. We shed lots of tears. We weren't at the funeral home for very long when we were all brought back outside, and our father spoke to all of us about those tears. He would not have it. Our tears would be too difficult for my aunt. We were to pull ourselves together. It wasn't the warmest way to do things, but if I reflect on that now, it was Dad's way of protecting his sister.

Overall, our home was emotionally warm. We had our best conversations in the living room or around the dinner table or over dishes. Mom was easier than Dad to talk to about things. Dad was more old school than Mom. Men shouldn't show emotion! Mom didn't show much emotion either, but she listened and allowed us to express our emotions for a bit. Once we processed something, her expectation was for us to then move on.

Our mom has such fond memories as a teenager that she enjoyed us as teenagers. She was excited about dances. She made clothes for us. She sewed a lot. She encouraged us to have our friends over before school events. When she became a grandmother, she enjoyed teenagers even more. She loved being around the kids and their friends. With her enthusiasm came an emotional warmth.

It was messy.

My Mom always said there was a difference between being tidy vs being clean or being messy vs being dirty. Our house was messy simply because of the amount of people all living in the same space. Not everything got put away all the time. We all shared cleaning chores, but the mess had to be picked up at least weekly. At times I remember that one of my Saturday jobs was to clean off the dining room table, and it would take me all day. It was the catch-all place for 11 people. It wasn't dirty, but there were many things out of place.

I remember the top of the fridge being very messy. There were receipts, and paper and coins. Sometimes there were chip bags and other snack bags on top of the fridge as well. I looked there every day to get loose change for the bus because that is where Dad emptied his pockets at the end of his workday.

The back entrance to the house was messy. Eleven people in and out everyday is bound to attract mess. It was a very small entrance, basically just a landing pad of 3' x 5' with stairs going down to the basement and steps going up to the kitchen and a small powder room off to the side. Imagine all of us in and out of that entrance: the shoes, the boots, the skates, the coats... I hated cleaning the back entrance.

The front entrance was messy. My dad used to ask all the time, "Why don't you come in the back door?" We didn't use the back door because the entrance was small. We all used the front door most of the time, it was more welcoming and coming in the front door brought us right into the hub of the house. We could see who was coming into the house from the living room so coming in the front door we felt like we got a bigger welcome. When grandchildren came along, and we would all gather at the house, the front entrance was crazy messy.

The kitchen was only messy at mealtime, or when Mom was making pies. The kitchen was clean, with almost nothing on the counter as everything was put away at the end of each day. Our parents couldn't rest unless the kitchen was clean. All of us now say we can't go to bed until our own kitchen is clean.

It was tidy.

We often had to tidy. Making things look clean was about picking things up and putting everything in its place. Sometimes we were required to do a quick "tidy up", but every Saturday my sister and I were on cleaning duty. Mom had returned to work. She worked a few evenings and Saturdays most of the time. Dad was in charge while Mom was at work. He was a grouch on Saturdays. He wanted us to clean things his way, but by the time he showed us his way, it was done, and we had just watched. He did the same to the boys with the lawn mower. They stood and watched his demonstration, and by the time he was finished showing them how to do it, it was almost done!

We were not allowed to make plans to go out with our friends on a Saturday until all our chores were done. Dad wanted the house clean for Mom when she got home from work.

We used to have one of those plastic runners over the carpet the ones with the little plastic spikes on them that helped them to stay in place. Ours spread from the front door to the kitchen. On one of our Saturdays, my sister and I were getting frustrated with Dad. If we were upstairs cleaning, he called us downstairs. When we came downstairs, he asked why we hadn't finished upstairs. The same sister that asked him if he had a piano tied to his leg is the one that flipped that runner over on that particular Saturday. We came upstairs, and then called him up, knowing he was in his sock feet and knowing that when he stepped on the runner he was likely going to swear! I am not sure that we have ever laughed together as hard as we did that day. Dad jumped and swore, and he couldn't muster any discipline because we were laughing so hard that he couldn't help but join us. Man, my sister was brave. She was younger, and our parents were a bit more relaxed, but she was fearless!

We managed to finish doing our chores, and he became less demanding. For many years after, we would remind him of this incident if he was giving us too many things to do at once. It always worked to get him off our backs as we got our work done.

It was spiritual.

We are a big Catholic family. Church was a non-negotiable way of life. We went every week, no matter what.

My dad often took 2–3 trips on a Sunday to accommodate all of us. We didn't necessarily all go to the same mass all the time, but we all had to go to church, and we had four options: Saturday night mass or three different mass times on Sunday.

Our parents knelt beside their bed every single night and said their prayers. There is a small church at the lake. Our holidays included one suitcase just for church clothes and going to mass on holidays was a must. Every Sunday there was a large bacon and eggs meal awaiting us upon our return from church; it was like a reward. We enjoyed church at the lake because we saw all of our cousins following the same tradition.

There was a crucifix in our home. Mom made sure each of us got one for a wedding gift as well. It was so important to her that we had our faith.

Our oldest cousin on our mom's side is a priest. We appreciate him and his spiritual guidance very much. He has accommodated the changes in generations while helping us all to hold onto our faith. As time has changed the way we honour our faith, our cousin has helped our parents and aunts and uncles to work through these changes. He helps the younger generations see the value in the traditions that were learned in earlier days.

My father died on August 28, 2004, on the day of Mom and Dad's 50th wedding anniversary. Our cousin said the funeral mass. It was comforting for all of us, but especially comforting for the younger generation. We left the church feeling like it was a beautiful day despite saying goodbye to our dad/papa.

My husband grew up in a faithful home as well. His parents had a church family, and he grew up with the same morals and values as I did.

My father-in-law died when our kids were 10, 12, 14, and 16. His funeral was huge and beautiful. The sheer volume of people in attendance was a comfort for our children. It was a time for them to be reconnected with their two cousins on my husband's side. It was difficult for the grandchildren to watch cancer take over his life, but they have no regrets of the time they spent with him prior to his death.

For my husband and I, giving our own children a foundation of faith to build on was our main goal as parents. We went to church often, and we tried to keep that as part of our family traditions as our own children became young adults. We led by example as much as we could, and we sent them through the Catholic school system because we knew we would need help on our journey as Catholic parents in an ever-changing world. Our children and grandchildren will not have the same spiritual upbringing that we did, but they are kind and spiritual and amazing human beings just the same. They work hard. They give back to their communities. They value their family roots, and they are proud of their Catholic education and faith.

When we tell the kids that their grandmas are praying for them, there is a sense of peace and comfort that fills their hearts, as they feel their grandmas have a close relationship to God himself.

It was a spiritual home.

For our children, although we went to church and tried to give them a faith base built on traditions and rituals like we were raised, we were more relaxed than our parents. We sometimes skipped going to church, and as our children got older, we allowed them to skip church. With shift work and all the activities of our four children, sometimes we felt that we needed to spend Sundays at home, with no morning rush and no church expectations. This is an area of extreme change from one generation to the next. Although we felt that our faith was important, we believed it was equally as spiritual to stay in the confines of our own home once in awhile and focus on being our own family.

CHAPTER #3

What I learned from my mom.

There are so many things I learned from my mom, and some of them I know I passed onto my own children, but some things I learned I didn't want to take with me into my parenting role.

I think one of the most important things I learned is to stand up for myself. If you want something, ask for it—the worst that can happen is that the answer will be "no."

My parents had a great relationship, as I remember it. There was obvious love and adoration, but there was also passion. Not just the kind of passion you think about when you think about love or sexual passion, although I do believe they had that too, but the kind of passion I witnessed was vivid in a discussion. My mom didn't bow down to my dad despite the times that they grew up in. She stood her ground, and she let him or us know if she was unhappy.

As we were all starting our married lives and people would say "never go to bed angry," my mom would disagree with that.

She said that sometimes you needed to have a night of unresolved thoughts so that you could process things and present your stand in the morning from a better platform. She said that if you are getting married, then your love is much greater than one night, so stand your ground.

I remember a story of a time when the house that we grew up in was being built. She was excited and wondered what it was going to be like. There was a similar house in another subdivision. Mom was very pregnant, but she went to that house and knocked on the door and simply asked, "Can I see your house? We are building a similar one and I want to know what it will look like." She was welcomed in and was then able to envision her new home. So, don't be afraid to ask, because the worst that can happen is that the answer will be "no."

Back to the thought of going to bed angry, I will admit that I have gone to bed angry. I feel that I do well to advocate for myself, and as a result I feel that my husband and I have left no stone unturned. I also know that he has gone to bed angry with me, but we have always been able to problem solve and move on.

Some of our parents' smaller arguments or heated discussions did happen in front of us. Those were the times that we learned about different emotions and how to manage them. We learned that it was okay to be sad, or mad, or frustrated, but what we never witnessed was physical or emotional abuse. We learned the art of negotiation, the ability to stop an argument (for the time being) and to re-visit it behind closed doors. We also learned that it was okay to argue, or have a discussion, and that everyone's opinion is important.

Presenting a united front is simply good parenting. Agree to disagree and stand together in front of the children for the children's sake. That being said, it is important to make the commitment to finish the discussion in private, resolve the issue, and move on.

My mom taught us how to cook. Our oldest son says she is the only woman in the world who can feed 20 people on a pound of ground beef. She learned to cook from her own mother. Like every other family, we all had our favourite things, and she worked tirelessly to keep us all happy. She did not stress over what we ate. She just didn't ever want us to go to bed hungry. To this day, she has a piece of toast and a glass of milk before she goes to bed, and when she stays with us, she has an uncanny way of making us feel like we should be doing the same, and we always seem to join her. She catered to our likes and dislikes. Mealtime was our family time. There were 11 people at the table night after night, and she just wanted it to be a nice time for us. If we didn't like what was being served, we could always have bread and butter, or in my younger brother's case, a hot dog! Yes, a hot dog. Often our Sunday dinner was roast beef. Many times, I can remember my brother coming to the table and asking nicely if he could have a hot dog, and nine times out of 10, Mom made him a hot dog. It was more important to her that we were all at the table than it was that we all ate the same thing. She made sure we had a vegetable and a fruit, she made sure we had meat, she made sure we had some dessert, but most of all she made sure we were full. That was the most important thing to her; she knew what that was like to be hungry as a child and didn't want it for us. She also did the best with what they had. Sometimes she didn't have enough fruit for all of us, but she had enough to make a pie, or she made jam squares because there was fruit in the jam.

My mother grew up poor. She talks about their home being so cold in the mornings that my grandmother stayed in bed when they got up for school. She didn't want that for us. She was up and making lunches every single morning that we had school. She didn't make lunches the night before because she wanted our lunches to be fresh. On a few occasions that she was ill or away and I was assigned lunches in the morning, all I remember is that it was a brutal, daunting task. All of those thoughts returned to me when I made my own kids' lunches, but I got up daily with minimal complaint and made them a fresh lunch daily... Oh how I loved Pizza Day!

I have five sisters. We all complain now about our bodies, our weight, our proportions, but none of us are overweight. Our body struggles I think come more from our father and his perception of what a woman should look like, or how she should keep herself, than they do from our mother. And interestingly, our Mom kept herself very well. By that I mean she was always dressed and showered. She took pride in her looks and her body. She liked to get dressed up, and I remember how good it felt when she was dressed up and looking her best. We were proud of her. We all learned the value in caring for ourselves and how that was important for the family. If Mom was sad or down, or looking like she was in a funk, we all felt it.

Our mom returned to work when our youngest sister started school. I remember her getting her own bank account and how important that was to her. She tells a story of wanting her own credit card and how she couldn't get one without my dad's signature. That wasn't good enough for her—she wanted her own! There is a small credit union in our town, and they gave her a credit card. Out of loyalty, she still does some banking with that credit union. I learned about perseverance and the value of having my own money and my own account from my mom.

Mom was practical. She helped when she could. She stood her ground when she needed to, she worked when she had to, and she was usually calm. This was a big deal. There were times when she was very mad at someone (usually the boys for playing hockey with sock balls in the living room) but she made a statement that included a consequence and if you pushed too hard then you paid the consequence. She was not much of a shouter, but if she said it, she meant it.

She was also practical when we were all starting families of our own. She would come to our homes and help when we brought a new baby home, but she came for a day, maybe two days, nothing close to this week or more visit thing like the kids have now. First, she was still working when grandchildren started to come along, and second, she would say, "This is your life. You created this, so you need to figure out what works for you. You will be great." And then she would leave. She left because she wanted to give us our space as we started our own family. She left because she respected that time as a couple and didn't want to interfere. She left because she had nine kids of her own, and she knew we would be just fine.

I remember when I brought our fourth child home, thinking I wanted her to stay forever. She didn't. My one older sister and I lived in the same small town about 45 minutes away from the rest of the family. I remember feeling like our kids weren't getting as much time with their grandparents as the other grandkids were getting and I was jealous. My jealousy was unfounded because it wasn't our kids who felt like they didn't get grandparent time, it was me. Our four kids all felt like they were her favourite. That was a gift my mother learned from her mother—making all the kids feel like they were the most important person in the world when they were with her.

When we were growing up, our parents did not tell us they loved us. As a matter of fact, I am not sure I ever heard it, though I did see it written on a card. I will say that there was never a time that I doubted how much I was loved. However, this was something I didn't want to take with me into my parenting journey. My husband and I were going to tell our kids we loved them every chance we got, and we did that. It was not that our parents didn't love us... it was just the way they were raised. There was nothing wrong with that, but it was something we wanted to change, and we changed it.

Unfortunately, we have been through some very difficult times as a family, both as a large extended family and also within our small family of six. We hear the words "I love you" more now than ever from my mom, and we cherish those words.

Along with saying "I love you" as much as we could, another thing I vowed to change was having conversations with our young adult children. My mom definitely said more to us girls than she did to the boys. She was very cautious with the boys and around their wives. I vowed that if I was going to discuss something that involved the family with my daughter then I was going to have that same discussion with my boys. I also vowed that if the boys could do it, then so could our daughter. We worked hard for our four kids to do equal chores, have equal opportunities, and have equal say. I would have to ask my kids to know if we were able to make that change, but my guess is that we did okay.

When Facebook became a thing, my mom wanted an account. She wanted to keep learning. She wanted to keep up with her grandchildren. She never wanted them to think she didn't know what they were talking about and as a result leave her out of a conversation. My mom likes to learn. She was always interested in what we were doing in school and was proud of our marks. She attended every graduation of every grandchild because she believes that learning is so important. Learning everyday is a great lesson.

I learned how to sew from my Mom. Sewing is my CALM, and as a result, I would say that sewing is one of the most important things I learned. My mom started showing me how to sew when I was 11 or 12 years old. I took Home Economics in grades 7 and 8 and did very well. She was able to help me with each project.

By the time I went off to college, I was sewing well on my own, and I used some of my student loan to purchase my first sewing machine.

I sewed for our kids and made many sets of curtains for our various homes. I made many repairs on clothing and sports uniforms for the kids. In 2004, after my father died, I decided to learn how to quilt. I had always loved quilts but didn't think I had the ability much less the time or money. I registered for a beginners' class and registered my mom in the same class. My thought was that it would be nice time to spend together. It was also an evening out for us, and I felt that would help us both with our grief process. Upon completion of the 10-week course, I finished a quilt and my mom made a table runner. She didn't love the quilting as much as I did, but the course did revive her love of sewing, and she started using some of her time to make housecoats and to do other small projects.

I found my CALM. I always loved to sew, but I really liked quilting. I like the planning and the choosing of colours. I love the entire process from beginning to end. Sewing and quilting allow me to forget about my stresses. I enjoy the "show and tell" part of a completed project. I like to complete small projects as well. I thank my mom often for giving me this gift.

CHAPTER #4

What I learned from my dad.

I think we all learned our competitiveness from our father. He was a great athlete, and he liked to win. We play lots of games at family functions and the strength and determination to win that comes forward can be a bit intense. When I was younger, maybe 10 or 12 years old, I would have said sports were for boys, not for girls. As we all worked on him, he mellowed, and he learned to be supportive of girls playing sports. I don't think any of my sisters would be upset if I made the statement that none of us are good athletes, and that's likely because we weren't encouraged athletically in any way. No disrespect to my dad, since he was just old school, and it's what he knew.

I also believe I got my sense of pride from my father. He was a very proud man, and sometimes his pride got the best of him. He was judgemental, and as we got older, we would get him pretty charged up if we talked about salaries of certain professionals. He took a strong stance on teacher and nurse salaries, for example. Teachers and nurses were human like the rest of us and didn't require such significant salaries. Oh, how the discussions got heated. But his pride forced him to stick to his thoughts, even though he didn't win those arguments! Thank goodness my sister-in-law loved him, because it seemed like he had most of the "nurses don't need that high of a salary" discussions with her.

He was very proud of his family. My mom says that there were times when people would tease them about having nine children, saying things like "Why didn't you guys get a television?" or "You know there is a thing called birth control?" As Mom remembers those comments, she says they were hurtful, especially for Dad. These comments made him sound like a "bad man," but he was not that. He was proud of what he had created, where they lived, and how we all presented as a family.

I remember when I was away at college and Dad had a meeting with the president of an investment company that worked with his firm. He called me and asked me to come for dinner with them. He felt the need to tell me to be dressed up and on my best behaviour. I was 18. I think I knew how to conduct myself! But I took his advice and was dressed up and on my best behaviour. I was pleased that he asked me to come but even more thrilled that I would have my dad all to myself, a rare occasion. This man who was with us at dinner wrote my mom and dad a letter telling them how impressed he was with me... what a nice thing to get in the mail for my parents and for me. I saw pride right before my own eyes, and it was for me, and it was a great feeling.

Our memories are built on family events. I remember my parents' 25th wedding anniversary and my cousin's ordination into the priesthood and his first mass. I remember family weddings, and of course, my wedding. In the photos taken at those events, you can see what pride is. It is vividly clear on my dad's face. One of my younger sisters was married after our dad passed away. When he was dying, she sat with him and assured him that she would be okay. Although he was unconscious, tears rolled down his face when she spoke to him. He was proud of her strength in that moment, but also sad, because he loved her as he did the rest of us and was sad to miss that moment with her. I also think he was letting her know he would be there when her day came. Her wedding followed a few years later, and there were many moments that beautiful day when it was evident his pride was shining on her.

As a side note, during the time in which he was very sick, my sister was in a fairly new relationship. The gentleman she was with had just purchased his first home. When he came to visit my dad in the hospital, he told my dad about his purchase. When he began to describe the house and the address, there was a silence that hung in the room for a moment. This man had bought my parents' old house, the one they lived in before they bought the bigger house in the new subdivision, the house that my sister was born in. In that moment, we saw pride. My dad was proud of this young man and proud to tell him that he had once owned that same house, and there was pride for my younger sister. It was Karma!

When we were young it seemed that Dad was a bit of a shouter, but he was a good sport, and as each daughter grew up and got braver, we challenged him, we mellowed him, and we helped him to adapt to new ways of thinking. Dad was proud of his boys as well. They had a different relationship with him than the girls did. He loved watching them skate. They are all such good skaters, and he loved to watch hockey in general, but he loved to watch his boys especially.

We learned our love of hockey from our dad. Friday nights were about watching hockey. We sat, we watched, and we didn't talk much, because hockey was on. We all sat on the floor or on a chair, and Dad had the couch to himself. He needed the entire couch because he had to move up and down the couch with the plays. He cheered, and he chirped the refs, but he loved hockey, and so do most of us. He would have loved to have been here for our billeting days. In Canada when a child is eligible to play junior hockey, they usually get drafted to a town different than the one they grew up in. The towns that had a team, had billets. Billets were families that took these boys into their homes and housed them during their hockey career in exchange for season tickets to all the home games and a small remuneration. We had the opportunity to have several boys live with us. It might not have been fun for the players, if my Dad was alive during this time because he would have had lots to say to them about the game and the way they played it. He would have challenged them on their style of play and would have loved to banter with them about the game, but at the same time he would have loved getting to know all those Junior players.

When grandchildren came along, he loved to hold them up high so he could get a good look at them. He especially liked them after a bath when they were all clean and smelled good. He loved to watch the kids growing up and playing together. He was in awe of their relationships and how happy they were to see each other. As the grandchildren became teenagers, they teased him, and he loved it. When those teenagers embraced each other each time they got together, he would often turn away to hide his tears. He was so proud of them and the relationships they had, and he knew he was responsible for some of that.

Dad was one of 12 children, and he had a brother who was one year older than him. Dad's brother was killed in 1948, at the section house that housed the coal tank for the engines near their home. The family was devastated. We know very little about Dad's brother because he could never talk about it. As we spent more and more time at the lake, only two kilometres from his family homestead, he often noted that the sound of the train whistle at the supper hour was one of the loneliest sounds in the world.

We learned about death and heartache at a very young age. We learned that it was a fact of life and that although it might affect you for the rest of your life, you should not allow that to affect your functioning. Life keeps going, and the most important thing to do is to embrace what is good and be thankful everyday.

My dad was feisty and fun. He was a shouter, and he was a grouch, but we learned at a very young age that his bark was worse than his bite. We knew he loved us, and we knew he was proud of us. We knew he adored his grandchildren and was a very proud man.

I realized soon after I was married that there are certain things, we take with us and certain things we leave behind. I wanted the father of my children to be less of a shouter. I wanted my children to feel free to talk to either parent without fearing the response. My husband and I had many conversations about the father role versus the mother role. We wanted to be more open to our children. We wanted our children to respect us like we were respectful of ours. We also wanted to earn that respect using a more positive parenting approach. We established a parenting strategy that was common to our generation: having more conversations with our children and giving them explanations and reasons for our decisions. We hoped to establish a parenting style that was less intimidating than what we grew up with.

In the early days of our parenting journey, coupled with my Early Childhood Education knowledge, we worked to make changes within our family.

My dad often challenged our style, but he was not critical. He grew up with more siblings than we had, and he raised more children than we were raising, but he tried to be respectful of the changing times.

CHAPTER#5

Our Parents

We learn so much from our parents and are influenced by them. The way we are parented, the way they cope with their emotions, and the way they manage their relationship all has influence on us as we grow up.

I know that in my family we all take something different from our family experiences. Our parents changed with each additional child. I am told that whether a family has 2 children or 10, each child takes something different and gives something different, and I can see that with our own 4 children. I wonder, is that because of the parenting changes or is that because of the uniqueness of each child? Interesting question isn't it especially when we all grew up in the same home.

As you grow into your adult life you realize there are things you can get away with depending on what parent you are working with at the time. We knew our Mom had the final say, but in her absence, we also knew Dad was more of a push over. I also know that our own children were quick to learn where they could push limits depending on which parent was in charge at the time. Our own children learned that I was able to manage chaos better than their Dad, I lived it, their Dad didn't and often didn't manage it well.

When we talk about raising children today, we talk about a structured predictable and consistent environment. We give advice in all areas, but its important to understand that all advice and education is given as a guideline and its important to understand that we all have a different framework to work from. Take what you can and then mold your information to work for your own family.

When we start a family its important to realize what influences us, and what influences our partner and then find a good blend of all things. From there we create our own family culture.

We learn about relationships from our parents. They guide us about parent child relationships and about brother sister relationships. We learn by watching them as they love, or fall out of love, we watch them manage our life and the people who come in and out of our life and we watch them as they manage their own sibling and friend relationships. At times we learn more by what we see than by spoken words. Some people don't have a good example and have witnessed abuse in different forms. Watching or learning in a harsh world must be very difficult. As adults, we can siphon what we learn, and take what we want that is good, and then work to be the best parent we can be.

CHAPTER #6

How things changed when I met my husband.

I failed Grade 11 math! What does that have to do with meeting my husband? Well, in 1978, when I was attending a Catholic high school and was in Grade 11, if you failed English or math you could go to summer school. Summer school was only offered at one high school in our small town, and it was not the Catholic one. I arranged to go to summer school and could only go if I could still work, because I had to work!

I went to summer school and had the best summer of my life! There was a big world of people, and opportunity, and friendships outside of my little Catholic school, and I have to say it was wonderful and changed my life. I'm not saying my high school was bad or awful, but there was so much more to explore.

I reconnected with a girl who I had met at Girl Guides. She was dating the most handsome guy in Belleville, and he attended a different high school in our town. I had heard about him, but had never met him, and all rumors were accurate about his looks. I hung out with them a little bit, and when the summer was over, we arranged to attend our local fair. Little did I know I would meet my future husband that night. He was with that handsome boyfriend of my friend, and he was just as handsome!

The other thing that happened that summer is that I met a guidance counsellor at the summer high school, and with some encouragement from him, I registered myself at that high school for my Grade 12 year and didn't tell my parents! Maybe I had picked up some of that bravery my younger sister had! I told my parents about my high school change on the holiday Monday before the start of the new school year. They were not happy. They worried about me being in such a big high school with no prayer and having a child not in attendance at "our" Catholic high school was so far out of their way of thinking. The summer high school was the pilot school for the first ever co-op program in Ontario. I wanted to be in that co-op program, and I wanted an opportunity to work with special needs children. Early into the program I got a placement at… are you ready for this title?… The William R. Kirk School for the Mentally Retarded.

The program was new, so the logistics were quite unorganized. I was registered at the summer high school, I attended classes two days a week at another high school at the opposite end of town, and I had placement at William R. Kirk. My parents did not have a clue where I was, and they didn't like it. I loved it.

I met so many new people and was now experiencing a different kind of high school life. I felt a new kind of freedom.

The best part is that my placement was beside the high school where my friend's boyfriend and my future husband went. I was soon invited to join them at lunch. I was invited to attend their football games with my friend and then my future boyfriend would drive us home. Before too long, he asked me to go out after a game to McDonald's just for a milkshake... and the rest is history.

I was 17 that year, and he was 18. He had one brother who was 10 years older, and I, of course, had what felt like a million siblings at that time in my life. It turns out that our parents knew each other, and my parents were comfortable with me dating him right from the start.

We had so much fun that school year. We watched football games and would just hang out. All four of us worked, and we all worked full time the following summer and met up almost every night after work. My husband was heading off to university, and I was unsure of what I might do, but I knew that visiting him at university was never going to be an option. I was allowed to go with his parents to drop him off, but under no circumstances was I allowed to visit him for his entire first year. There was no FaceTime at this time, and we had no long-distance plan... we wrote letters and made plans for every third weekend for him to return to our hometown and that's when we saw each other.

At the start of his second year, and the start of my first year at a community college in another town, we knew we wanted to be together. We talked about it all the time. On August 28, 1981, in his parents' kitchen while they were away, he proposed to me after cooking a steak dinner.

I SAID YES.

We were so excited, but our parents were less so. We were young, too young. What about school? Why did we need to be engaged? Both of us were adamant that we would not make any wedding plans until we were both finished school. I had never been away from home, and I felt like I needed some freedom for awhile. We both talked about all kinds of things for our future, and none of those conversations included a wedding until we each had completed our schooling. We felt that was a very good decision on our part, but the "too young" thing was a constant phrase that was thrown at us. One of my older sisters, although she tried to be happy about my engagement, made it very clear that I would not be getting married before her. She wasn't even engaged at the time, but I guess because she was older, she wanted to be married first. She got married the summer before we did.

My husband's parents wanted him to become a doctor or a lawyer. They wanted him to have more education. They worried that our relationship would prevent him from going further in school. My parents worried about our age because I was younger than my older siblings making this commitment to a married life. It was difficult for us to stay on our course to get married, but we never wavered from our plans to finish school first and to marry immediately upon completion. Being in separate cities for most of our post-secondary life allowed us to have separate conversations with our parents so that when we were together, we could discuss our plans and sort through some of the negative influences. Our time together in those years was minimal, so we invested more time into making plans that made us happy rather than spending it talking about our parents' worries.

We often talk to this day about how different things are for our kids than they were for us. We had an obligated obedience with our parents. We were engaged and then married and still we took a significant amount of direction from both of our parents. That is one thing we didn't want for our kids. We really wanted them to be able to make decisions of their own and chart their own course. No disrespect to our parents, but sadly we don't have fond memories of them being excited or happy or supportive in the same way that we were with our kids, a sign of different times.

Our wedding was amazing. I think there were 12 weddings that year between both sides of the family, and ours was the last one. We were married on the Friday night of Thanksgiving weekend in 1983. My maid of honour was one of my first cousins. She was always my favourite person and remains so to this day. She is just one of those people who I aspire to be like; she is content all the time, she never asks for more, and she is always

CALM. Our best man and his wife are dear friends, and we have shared a lifetime of memories with him and his family to this day. My youngest brother and sister were also in our wedding party, and a little girl who I babysat was our flower girl. I turned 21 two weeks after we got married; we were young, and we were totally okay with that.

We worked hard, we knew what we wanted, and we had big plans for a family and a life of our own. Our first child arrived two weeks after our first anniversary, and we brought him home on the day of my 22nd birthday. We had many conversations about building a family and decided that we wanted our children close together, so we had three more children all two years apart. We had four kids under six at the ages of 28 and 29 respectively and we planned it that way. No regrets.

When we were first married, my husband worked for his father as a painting contractor. We lived in a small, two-bedroom apartment in the same town as our families. We saw our parents a lot, maybe too much, and maybe that's why they influenced us so much. They knew a lot about our life. There were expectations, and we met them. It never crossed or minds to say no to them about attending Sunday dinners, or about working extra hours, or about wanting to go someplace for a weekend and being told that was a crazy idea and so we didn't go! They had so much influence on us, and we made sure that our own children did not experience the same.

Our first opportunity to move to a different town came in 1987. We would move to a small village about 30 minutes from our nation's capital. We had a two-year-old and a three-month-old baby, what were we thinking moving away from all our supports? Well, we did it. We moved away, and as hard as it might have been, it was a very good experience, and to this day we have a strong admiration for that small village and the people we met at that time in our lives and remain connected to. We stay mainly connected with a family who have a child the same age as our youngest child, and they help us to stay connected to the rest of the village. This move was the start of us making our own decisions. We made decisions and then informed our parents of our plans; we didn't consult them before we made the decision. I usually informed my parents and my husband informed his. This decision to talk to our own parents worked for us, as it seemed easier to handle their worries and talk them through with our own parents. When these conversations were finished, we then shared with each other. We moved several more times after that, and this strategy of sharing information with our own parents separately worked well for us.

In our married life, we always talked about having our own piece of property on the lake. We were given the opportunity to buy a piece of property in 2006. We built small sheds on the property. The sheds were all insulated and drywalled and we developed an amazing cottage atmosphere. We often talked about building a dream home but didn't think we could live "so far out." We always said we might someday build a cottage "but we will never live here." My husband also said he would never work in Toronto, but in 2015, he was offered a job to work in Toronto and the company offered to provide an apartment to us in Toronto. What a fun time in our life—it was like we were first married! We had so many fun times in that little apartment.

As the saying goes, "Never say Never!" Chris worked in Toronto for two years, and in 2016, we sold everything, moved into the basement of my mother-in-law's condo and worked to build our dream house on the lake, which is where we live now, and it isn't "too far out." We love living here.

With many ups and downs—though mostly ups—we have been married for 35 years and are still counting. We continue to dream together and work everyday at our marriage and are forever thankful for all the blessings that have been bestowed upon us.

CHAPTER #7

Four kids under six.

At 28 years old, I had four kids under six and loved being a mother. We talked at great length about the kind of family we wanted, including the age difference we hoped to have between our children, and we talked about being young parents. I talked more than my husband about numbers, but originally felt that six kids was a great number.

Before we were married, I went to the doctor to discuss birth control (a conversation that was not discussed in our home). I was a virgin when we got married, and birth control was not a Catholic thing. I kept it quiet but decided that I would not go to hell if I took birth control. It was a time in our life when we were making decisions that suited us, our relationship, and our new married life.

We were married in early October, and I found out I was pregnant in late March. Yep... I got pregnant on the pill. I learned very quickly that pregnancy was not my friend. I was sick for most of the nine months every single day, often four or more times. The fun parts were that we were having a baby, and my sister was pregnant as well, and our due dates were off by less than a week.

Our first born came along on October 20, 1984, two weeks after his cousin. The cousin bond of these two started in utero. We brought him home on the day of my 22nd birthday. We were young, but not too young! It was our journey, and we were excited. Our parents were excited about this baby, especially when they saw him, but struggled to instill in us that we had the ability to be good parents at such a young age. It was at this time in our life where we felt that "obligated obedience." If we said we were going somewhere for the weekend, they would voice their discontent, which often changed our plan. We did go to my husband's university to see his buddies when our baby was only five weeks old despite our parent's desire for us not to make that trip. It was liberating for us. We talk about that weekend to this day. It was the start of our independence as parents. It was a process, and it took many CALM conversations charting our own course and learning to stand our ground.

One of the best pieces of advice we ever received in our parenting journey came from our family doctor. Our family doctor was the father of our best man. He was my family doctor growing up, and we knew him socially. I was in to see him for one of our baby's appointments, and I began to cry because I felt like our parents were overbearing and didn't give us enough credit as parents.

He said this: "You need to have enough faith in yourselves as parents to do what works best for you. This isn't about your parents; it's about you and your husband and what you want for your family. Acknowledge your parents' comments, but you don't have to do what they say. You are parents now, so do what works for you." And then he added, "I think you are doing an amazing job, and I think you have great instincts. Trust that."

We never forgot those words, and we have passed them on many times to many friends and young people who are feeling inadequate or who might be struggling with their parenting journey.

In the early days of this journey we were in a two-bedroom apartment, and we had great neighbours in that apartment. It was an old building, so we could hear them, and they could hear us. They were very supportive and excited about our first born. We visited back and forth a lot. The proximity of the neighbours and the constant back and forth visits was a CALM for us. They were a consistent support, and we have good memories of that first apartment.

When we talked about our family after our son was born, we decided that we would not use birth control, and we would let things happen as they did. Our second child was born two years and four months after the first. A little girl. Now we had one of each.

At that time, there was so much information coming out about bonding. Being an Early Childhood Educator, I was very interested in newborn bonding. I was overwhelmed, uninformed, and under-educated about birthing with our first. I wanted a different experience with our second child. I approached this subject with our family doctor, and although he was aware of the research, he knew my ideas of bonding and nursing on the delivery table would not be well received. Our community hospital was not exactly keeping up with this new research. We pushed, and he agreed that for us to not have to turn our baby over to the nursery immediately and to be able to experience "skin to skin," he would have to be in the room when the child was born. We had his private number, and when our second child was close to her arrival, my husband slipped out and called our family doctor. She was born February 12, 1987. Our family doctor arrived at the hospital just before she arrived and upset the entire birthing floor! Even he had to justify his presence to the nurses, and we were scolded for calling him.

The bonding experience was so great, and it was all thanks to him for believing in us, and for allowing us to do things our way. He is a good man, and we remain connected to him and cherish our relationship with him as a man who had such a positive influence in our lives.

When our second child was three months old, we moved about three hours away from family for my husband to start a career with a large dairy plant. Our parents were nervous again. We would be far from home, far from them, and supports would be few in a new community. Little did they know that the supports in this small village were amazing. The entire village embraced our little family. Our parents visited occasionally, and we travelled home once every month or so.

At this time, there were many books being published about relationships and families. We did lots of reading because we wanted our children to build relationships with their cousins and proximity was not on our side. These books informed us about creating memories and traditions. They informed us about taking responsibility for building rituals into our family life and how these rituals would enhance relationships.   The hardest part about living away from our hometown was that my siblings were having children and our kids were only able to see their cousins on occasion. We travelled to the lake much more often than we travelled to our parents' home. At the lake, there were lots of cousins and little ones, and the cousin bond soon had a solid foundation to grow on. We realized that if we wanted our children to have these relationships, we would have to do all the travelling. It seemed that making that trip to the lake was easier for our family to travel than to ask eight other families to travel our way. Although at times we were frustrated at the lack of visitors to our home, we embraced the responsibility of creating rituals with our family, and we built great memories.

My mother- and father-in-law also had a cottage at this time. We were able to be close to the water no matter where we visited and so began our discussions about someday having a lakefront property.

In August of 1987, my parents bought their own piece of property on the lake and began to build their cottage. Minimal architectural plans, nine kids, 10 grandchildren and more to come, and the idea that after the shell was built, we would ALL help to finish the cottage as they could afford to do so. These were fun times.

During Easter of 1988, I did not feel well. Probably because we would soon be having our third child. I was 26 years old. This one was due Christmas Day. Clearly unplanned... who plans a baby at Christmas? Number two and Number three would be less than two years apart. We were excited and nervous and needed to have more discussions. In this small village where we lived, there was no such thing as an epidural. I was uncomfortable not having the option. I wanted a referral to the nearest larger center, which was in our nation's capital. This was a big deal because of the time of year. We would need someone on standby, and weather was never predictable. After some strong discussions with our doctor, we were able to plan to deliver at a bigger hospital about 30 minutes from our home. Our third child was born December 21, 1988, at 11:36pm. He missed being born on his paternal grandmother's birthday by less than 30 minutes.

He was born in a very up-and-coming hospital. There was no argument or fight for bonding; in fact, he was in my room for the duration of my stay. The other two children came to visit him, as did my aunt and my mother-in-law. Everyone could hold him, and that was a new experience for us. We brought him home on Christmas Eve with an almost two-year-old and a four-year-old anxiously awaiting the arrival of Santa Claus. This was a chaotic time. A nice time, a blessed time, but a chaotic time.

We decided that we had so much to be thankful for that we should go to church that Christmas Eve. The priest at the time greeted us at the entrance, and when he realized that our baby had been born, he dared to ask if he could carry our new baby up the aisle. This baby would represent "Baby Jesus." I let him carry our new baby. He allowed our other two children to be part of that procession as well. I must say, it was a pretty cool experience. I was dying on the inside with anxiety and was not prepared to let someone hold my new baby so soon, but at the risk of spreading my anxiety, I allowed it, and to this day our son reminds his siblings that none of them were ever asked to be a "Baby Jesus."

Our third birth was complicated in many ways. We had many challenges with the pregnancy and the delivery. The complications stayed with me for over a year and included some surgeries. Our third child was also sickly. Our doctor suggested that getting pregnant again anytime soon would not be good. He suggested that my body needed a rest, and so we were back to the birth control conversation. It needed to be a strong one because this young family started sooner than we might have planned while using birth control. We made a second attempt at using birth control.

In April 1990, our third child was very sick. He was hospitalized, and we almost lost him. I had never seen a doctor with that kind of fear on his face. He stayed with us at the hospital until the wee hours of the morning. He was scared, and so was I. We had never known that kind of fear and hope to never feel it again. This was another time when I had to stand my ground to do things my way. Our baby was laying in a crib, restrained, and hooked up to an IV. There was no touching him. I couldn't handle it any longer. I took him from the crib, I held him close, I fed him from a syringe, and he soon began to rally. He was released from the hospital a week later, and so began the process of "rebuilding" him. He was frail, and he had to learn to walk all over again. He was a fussy baby, and he stuck to me like Velcro.

In August 1990, I discovered that I was pregnant. My husband had accepted a new job in a new community about four hours away but closer to our hometown. Our third child was slowly getting better but giving this body a rest wasn't going to happen!

These were chaotic times.

We had neighbours at that time who had a child the same age as our third child. Their little boy was also admitted to hospital when ours was. Their little boy was a tank. He was a sick boy, but he was so much bigger and stronger that he rallied much quicker. We had such great times with this family. They both worked shift work, and I often cared for their boy. We had meals together and spent endless nights hanging out in our backyards. This is where we found our CALM. Moving away from them was very hard. Oh, how I wanted them to move with us because of the friendship and happy times we shared. We remain friends with them and with other friends that we met in the small village.

But we had to move on. We moved to another small town, bigger than the previous one, but still a small town. There was a new doctor in town who was our age and being new to this town as well we already had some things in common. This doctor and his wife became dear friends and started a network of people that stands as a strong network to this day.

This young doctor would deliver our fourth child. Our child was the fourth delivery for his practise and the first boy he delivered in our new town. Our fourth child was born on February 14, 1991, and despite the challenges for this body of mine, he came without any problems and was an easy and very pleasant baby. In our family, the saying goes, "nice o baby."

His brother, the previous youngest, was not happy about his arrival at first. He waited at the front door for several days, waiting for "the mom" to come and get "it." After all we had been through, our third child was not interested in sharing his mama.

Insert the start of many challenging behaviours. Our third child was tough enough that our parents would ask us to separate the kids if we asked them to look after them. Hearing "I can take him (Number three), but not with the others" or "I can take the other three, but not with him," became common.

This is the time in our life when we sought counselling. Our third child challenged us daily. We noticed we were shouting more, and we felt like we had lost whatever CALM we might have had. We knew we needed help. Parenting trends were changing. The parental advice we were being given didn't match the trends. We did more reading and were eager to learn about his behaviours and how to manage them. It was during our counselling that we were encouraged to stop shouting. We were encouraged to try to understand the needs of our family emotionally. We were encouraged to make decisions that worked for our family. We were encouraged to create traditions and rituals and to bring more positive energy into our home. The trend was positive parenting. CALM parents = CALM children.

Our third child struggled for the next several years to find his place in the family. He was so much fun and full of energy, and he was also sickly at times. His illnesses and behaviours halted many plans, and he required both of us to be "on" all the time.

Our fourth child was calm and easy... thank goodness. With new strategies and a commitment to parent together, we re-gained our CALM. A friendship soon grew between our two youngest boys, who eventually became inseparable.

We worked hard at raising our family. We learned to create traditions and rituals that worked for us. We learned to stand our ground. We learned the importance of self care and of marital care. We learned that it was hard work, we learned to work through chaotic times, and we worked always to find a CALM. It was hard, and it was awesome.

We employed a young teen as a babysitter. We asked her to come to our home to help sometimes and to babysit at others.

We learned in our counselling sessions the value of taking time as a couple. We learned that working together and showing our children a strong parental unit was also giving them a sense of security and stability. This was hard work, but we started to feel confident in our parenting style, and we were very proud of our little family. During one of our couple times away from the children, we decided that we would not have anymore children. Our plates were full. Financial pressure was hard to manage on top of trying to raise a family in general. My husband was only 30. Getting a doctor to agree that it was okay for us to do something permanent about birth control was a challenge. These were the times when "standards" started to be published. Everything had an average age, and the health ministries had published guidelines about certain things. This was another moment when we had to stand our ground. We had made a decision that was right for us, and with some more discussion with our doctor friend, we made a permanent decision to not have anymore children.

Making decisions that worked for us was difficult. Our ability to stand our ground and make decisions felt like we were betraying our parents. We made so many great friends along the way and soon learned that we were not alone in our search for our own parenting style or in our feelings of betrayal. Having such a great network of friends who were all experiencing the same challenges was very helpful during these times. We were called the "sandwich generation." We all struggled to make the jump from how we were raised to how we wanted to raise our children, and some of the generational changes were big. We found strength and CALM spending time with our own friends and making sure we invested time in our marriage and in our extended families.

The next 25 years were about raising this family, enjoying the moments, working through the struggles, and creating lifetime memories.

These years did not come and go without heartache and struggle, but there were more happy, fun, and great experiences than anything else.

CHAPTER #8

Looking back.

The moves, the friendships, the Ice Storm, the sacrifices we made, billeting and Evac.

When I look back over the years of raising this family and working in Child Development and Mental Health, I am easily triggered by certain things. Certain houses that I see remind me of houses we had. We had brand new homes and older homes. We had small homes and a few bigger homes. The consistent memory is that we loved our homes. We made them ours. When we rented and were restricted about decor, we were still able to make the homes our own. Being a huge fan of photographs, each home had many photographs that included pictures of previous places we lived and always included baby pictures because we had such adorable babies. When you take pride in your home, your children will do the same.

Each time we moved we celebrated it as an adventure. It was important to us that the kids understood that we would work hard to maintain friendships from all the places we lived. They were being asked to leave their friends, their schools, and their lives as they knew them to accommodate career changes. This was hard for them, but when we celebrated it, we felt like it made it easier for them. We rented halls, hosted parties, and allowed them to invite their entire classes. We took pictures and celebrated the adventure. It got harder as they got older, but in 1999, when we moved back to our hometown, the celebration was critical in making this a positive move.

Our oldest child was 16 years old. We were moving him halfway through Grade 11, halfway through a semester, and taking him from a long-term relationship with a girl. It was a hard time for him.

Our daughter was in Grade 8. She would only have half the year with the kids in her new school before she would go on to high school. She did not like us or anything about this move. She was friends with a beautiful family in the town we were living in. They had three girls and a boy, the opposite of us. These girls were dynamic; they were part of a dance team, and they were on a cheerleading team. They introduced our daughter to cheerleading, and she was hooked. Like really hooked! She was so in love with cheerleading that she couldn't imagine her life without it, and we were telling her that we were moving back "home" to a town that had no cheerleading. She hated our guts!

These were chaotic times.

Our third born was up for the adventure. His energy was such that he accepted the "adventure" and was keen to move on.

This was a time in our life and in his life when he was probably the easiest one to manage.

Our youngest was excited about the parties that would celebrate our move but not excited about the move itself. He was showing signs at that time in his life of anxiety, and he suffered migraines. The migraines got progressively worse during this time, and he developed mono. It was also at this time that we discovered he had a "Constitutional Growth Delay." His size was 5.9 years behind his chronological age. We knew he was small, but 5.9 years was a lot. We had many trips to The Hospital for Sick Children and eventually he became the great athlete that he wanted to be—a small athlete, but a great athlete—and he loved his time in our hometown.

We have friends all up and down the 401 corridor. We have worked hard to maintain these friendships. Our friends have children the same age as all or most of our children. Although they may not see all these kids all the time, the bonds of friendship are something that we taught our kids that we are proud of.

Both of our parents, the kids' grandparents, instilled in us the value of friendship, and we have been able to pass that on.

My mother- and father-in-law both come from a much smaller family than my parents. They surrounded themselves with so many friends. Their friends became their extended family. For my parents, their friends were mostly family. There was so many of them all the same age that they were able to build friendships with cousins and brothers and sisters.

Our kids have built relationships with friends and with family, and, as a result, have a huge network of people that they are connected to and we are proud of that.

One of our moves put us in another small town near our nation's capital. We lived there for four years, and they were probably the hardest four years of our married life. We had a great house. We loved that house, and the families we met there, but we never quite felt like we fit in. Everyone we met were lifers in that community and we weren't.

The most significant memory in this town was living through the Ice Storm. It was a famous Ice Storm. We had a chimney fire, so we had to leave our home, and we had only lived in this town for six months... Where on earth would we go?

Well, one of the families we met had two kids the age of our oldest two kids. They were that kind of family that embraced all of us, and our kids loved any opportunity to go to their home, so when the ice storm happened, we accepted their invitation to live there. Those were the first days of call display on the phone. The morning of the storm, while still in our home, I had to call the fire department because we had a chimney fire, and I could see bits of siding from the house engulfed in flame going by the window. My husband was a volunteer firefighter at the time, and he always said that one of his fears was that he would get a call someday and it would be to his home address, and his fear was about to come true. With no power, I attempted to call him at work, but pushed the wrong button and called my parents. They were watching the news but didn't realize we were being affected by this storm. My mom answered the phone very casually because she could see that it was me. When I heard her voice, I do believe I swore, "Oh, shit! I didn't mean to call you, Mom. We have a house fire. I will call you back." And then the phone lines went out.

These were chaotic times.

We moved into town with the family that offered us a place to stay. We brought whatever finger food we had, and we brought pajamas and a change of clothes each. It was not a big home, and there were six of us, so we packed light. We played the board game called "Sequence" for the next six days and will likely never play that game ever again. We were safe there. After we settled in, I realized that I had hung up on my mother and made a call back to my parents. This call back was difficult because as they imagined our stress, they continually suggested that we drive to their home. They believed that they could offer more help if we were closer. They were not understanding the magnitude of this event. Our vehicle was frozen in the garage and the authorities were asking people to stay off the roads. We stayed with our new friends for six days until the stack came off their house and we all had to move. We moved in with another family and after three days there we accepted our parents' advice and headed for our hometown. Seven days with no shower and four uprooted kids... get me out of here!

We had to put our fire plan into gear for the first time ever. We had to live with another family at a stressful time. We learned that having tons of food in a large freezer was useless, that food is not much good to you if the power goes out and it all goes bad.

We learned the value of being surrounded by good people.

Debit machines were new at that time, and they all went down during the Ice Storm, so we learned to hide cash in the house for emergencies.

We learned to not take anything for granted.

We have some great memories from the Ice Storm. These were chaotic times, and they made great memories.

These four years were financially our most difficult years, and the company my husband worked for did not stand true to their word on creating a career plan for him that was suitable for our family.

We moved to this town in May. My husband went ahead of us by six weeks. The week that I arrived with four kids in this new town, my husband shared that this company was moving him to a permanent midnight shift. Thank goodness the friends we met were such a great support. We travelled to the lake many times over the next four years. The lake was the one thing that was consistent and comforting. It was our CALM.

This same company wanted us to move to the United States after four years. It was a great opportunity for my husband, but not so much for myself or for the kids at the ages they were. The company wasn't willing to commit to more than two years, and the stress was huge. At the same time, the same dairy company that he had worked for when we were first married offered us the opportunity to move back to our hometown, and so we did.

My father-in-law lost his battle with cancer a year to the day after we moved home. We were happy to have that year with him, and we were especially happy for him to have that time with his grandchildren. It was a good move, even if it may have taken us some time to realize that.

Being from such a large family and having built such great friendships, it was a big deal to move. I had a sister living 45 minutes west of our parents, but the rest of our siblings all lived in our small town. Leaving that small town was a big sacrifice. We were leaving familiarity, friends, family and a comfort level.

We put our kids through many moves, but looking back on those moves, we felt like we helped our children learn about friendships, opportunity, and resiliency. We missed Sunday dinners; we missed some cousin times. We missed adult times, and we missed our friend

My husband and I were happy to move back to a place that we always referred to as home. Over the next eight years, we sacrificed our privacy and always seemed to have someone extra in our home. We had my cousin for a year. A few times we had one of the kid's friends, and at one time we housed a colleague of my husband's.

When our youngest kid was the last one at home, we had the opportunity to billet for our local Junior A hockey team.

This was not an experience we had ever thought about; it was an opportunity that seemed to fall upon us. My youngest sister was billeting and heard that there was a need for more billets. She asked us to contact the hockey organization and with excessive encouragement from our youngest son—who did not like being the only child in the home—we decided to try billeting. The first kid to come into our home became very near and dear to us. He was a good kid and very respectful. He was needy, but not in a bad way. He was always appreciative and liked being cared for. We had him for one-and-a-half years. Over the next eight years, we had a total of 12 players live with us. We had only one bad experience with billeting, and some of the players keep in touch with us. We continued to billet long after our kids were gone. It might seem like we sacrificed our privacy and our chance to be on our own, but truth be told, I wasn't ready to be empty nested. During these years, my husband was away a lot, and having these players was a good time for us and gave us lots of good memories.

We had a young Italian player who was awesome, and a young man from Denmark who was with us for six months. The last player to live with us was with us for three-and-a-half years; he was like one of our own, he was our fifth child. That last year, we had two boys together and they were great together. We played a lot of cards that year and had lots of "beauty club" dinners. These boys were good to us and we were good to them.

Leaving each town and starting over was hard work. It was hard to leave the networks we created and hard to start new ones. It was hard to watch the kids struggle and exciting to watch them create new friendships.

As each of our kids moved away, they didn't seem to struggle as much as some of their peers. They had experienced moving and knew that they could make new friends. They knew the value of building new resources, and they became good at it, so going away and having a post-secondary experience did not seem as difficult for them as it was for their peers.

After we finished billeting and our own kids were all on their way, we had some decisions to make. My husband was working in Toronto, and I was in the house alone, so we only saw each other on the weekends. Sometimes he came back to the house and sometimes I went to Toronto for the weekend. We didn't need our big house, and this was our time, so what did we do next?

In 2016, we decided that it was time to sell the house and make our move. We decided that we would move to the lake if everything lined up as we hoped.

I made a promise to our daughter-in-law that when she had to return to work after our first grandchild was born, that if she wanted I would take a leave from work and go to stay with them for two months to assist her in getting her groove back to work. I felt that it was important for her to get settled before they had to worry about getting their first born settled into a day-home situation. She accepted my offer.

Our oldest son and his wife and first born live in Northern Alberta. I couldn't imagine getting a baby out the door early on a cold winter morning. My leave of absence was accepted, and I went there for two months. Our house was for sale, and we would make plans to move if everything fell into place.

At the end of my two-month stay, I ended up evacuating with our children during the fires in Fort McMurray, Alberta. It was the largest Canadian natural disaster, and the second scariest thing I had ever lived through, after I thought we might lose our third child. This was the same kind of fear I felt when we were evacuating. There were a few times when I thought we would die in the fire. There were 65,000 people all evacuating at the same time. I was in the car with my oldest son, his wife, and our first grandchild, and I was helpless. I had absolutely no control, and it was a very difficult situation. During the evacuation, our real estate agent called to say that there was an offer on the house. I really didn't care, and he couldn't understand my lack of interest. Once he remembered where I was, he realized the reason for my lack of interest and took over everything. The house sold during the evacuation!

The memories of this event can still bring me to tears. Our youngest son and his girlfriend (now his wife) were ahead of us by about two kilometres in the evacuation. Our youngest son minimized the seriousness of this event shortly before there was a call for a mandatory evacuation. It was a very difficult time for me to remain calm as a parent. Thankfully we talked about that conversation after we made it to safety and acknowledged that conversation was driven by fear.

Our daughter was about six hours from us, and we were headed to her home for safety. Our third child was in London, Ontario, and my husband was in Toronto. I have never felt so disconnected, and yet we were all in touch minute-by-minute, and we got through it.

That six-hour distance to our daughter's home took us over 12 hours of driving. Our grandson slept through most of the drive. I will never forget the look of fear on my son and daughter-in-law's faces as we drove down the road with fire on both sides. I will never forget the feeling of being held by my daughter when I arrived at her home and telling her how scared I was thinking I would never lay eyes on her again. I will never forget seeing my husband after the evacuation and not wanting to let him out of my sight. I will never forget the greeting of our Ontario son when I returned home. I will never forget that fear and the gratitude I felt for our safety and the safety of the entire community.

My role as a mother was so very different during this time. I felt like I didn't know how to parent in this moment. I also realized that, agree or disagree, my son and his wife were making the decisions for their family, and I was tagging along. I offered suggestions for a plan and then waited for them to let me know how they wanted to proceed. Parenting your child who is a parent himself is hard. Your role changes. Your children aren't children anymore; they are adults. When do I talk? Is it better to just sit silently? When do I advise? When do I take a backseat? These are all things our own parents must have struggled with. The difference is that we were in crisis, and I needed to remain CALM. I believe that during this time our relationship changed, and we became peers. We were able to draw on our past and have a positive dialogue where we established and executed a plan to get out of town safely.

This was a chaotic time.

The support of family and friends was incredible. The support of people who knew our daughter and knew that we had evacuated to her home was immeasurable. The support of our son-in-law who stayed connected to me, and the calls from my siblings and friends as we knew we were safe was a great comfort. This support was where we found our CALM.

The sacrifices were many, the lessons were big, the memories were amazing, and all of these are the things that make us who we are today.

CHAPTER #9

Roots and wings for all of us.

"Roots and wings, Leslie. Roots and wings."

This was a statement made to me one night when I was out with work friends. Everything was changing, and I was struggling.

I love the roots part, but I wasn't sure I wanted them to have two good wings. I wasn't sure I wanted them to leave, but I was sure that I wanted them to be strong, independent, good humans.

We wanted this. We wanted them to have more than we did. That doesn't mean we didn't have enough; it's just that we wanted them to be able to have more opportunities. We didn't want them to experience that same obligated obedience that we felt we were held to. We wanted our kids to go where they wanted to go. We wanted them to make their own decisions, and we wanted them to do what they wanted to do, whatever that was. We wanted them to never forget where they came from, and we wanted them to never lose their love for each other. It was so important to us that our kids would be good friends.

We were so proud of every milestone they achieved. We were proud when they made big plans, and we tried to support everything they did. We never wanted them to feel like they weren't capable because we knew what that felt like, and we didn't like it.

Working in mental health from the time our oldest child was 12, I learned so much about being emotionally sound. I had great training in crisis management and in behaviour management. I learned about work/life balance, and the best part of my work was my colleagues. When you work with the same people everyday for 16 years, those people end up becoming your work family and sometimes your greatest supports.

My husband was affected by three corporate downsizes. Three times he was walked out the door of his workplace due to cuts. The first two times my work family kept track of me and made sure I was emotionally okay. My work family saw me through the death of my father and the changes in our family as our kids moved onto their post-secondary school lives. They saw me through boyfriend and girlfriend grief, they supported my life as a high school cheerleading coach, and on and on.

On one occasion, one of my colleagues approached me at lunch hour. It was the Monday after I had dropped my youngest child off at college. She simply asked me how I was doing, and I fell apart. As always, the entire staff gathered, and we talked through that lunch hour at great length. I was not shedding tears of sadness because our last child had left the nest, but it was the realization that our family dynamics were forever changed. We were so proud of him and wanted him to have this experience, but I knew from this point forward that our time together as a family would require planning and coordination, and truthfully, I wanted to go back to having four little children that I could put to bed in my house and know exactly where they were.

My work family was an incredible support. My work also gave me satisfaction. Living in a small town, it's common to run into people who have been in your office and who needed help. It's nice to run into clients in our local retail stores, or while out shopping, and they appear clearly happy to see you. Those are satisfying times when you feel like you have been helpful. Some of the parents that I was able to help remain in our small town, and it's always nice to see them.

I will always remember my return to work after the evacuation from the Fort McMurray fires. I went into my workplace prior to my return date because I knew emotions would be big, and I knew we would all need some time together. It was a very emotional reunion. I was vulnerable, and they were there for me. I had just experienced a trauma, our house had sold, we had three weeks to pack up 20 years, we were moving into the basement of my mother-in-law's condo, and I needed to return to work.

These were chaotic times, but I had come to the realization that my workplace was my CALM. My colleagues were my CALM. The planning for our dream house on the lake was my CALM.

I knew we would be okay. I knew we had to get through it, and I knew we would.

Chaos is a crazy thing. It is not considerate of your state of mind or the activity level in your home or family. Chaos will enter your life at any time, on any day, and for any multitude of reasons. Chaos does have a negative connotation to it, but in my experience, it can be positive and negative. Chaos is a birthday party for a one-year-old or for a 90-year-old. It is a process not going as it should. It is too many things or too many people all needing your attention at one time. Chaos is getting a family organized to get out the door at the same time or bringing them all back in that same door after a big event. Chaos is the first day of school, the unknowns, the new clothes, a new school, new friends, new teachers, new processes, or a new bus route. It is the last day of school, the anticipation of freedom and summer holidays. It is the organization of a family because not everyone has the summer off. Chaos is major holidays, loving them or not. It rears it's head in many different forms. The key for us was to find our CALM and then face the chaos together with a plan.

In a time frame of less than one year, our dream of living on the lake was beginning to be a reality. The contractors broke ground on January 9, 2017. Due to ministry cuts, the clinic where I worked at was slated to close on January 16, 2017. My husband was affected by corporate downsizing on March 2017 for the third time in our married life. We had to clean out and give up the apartment in Toronto, and we had no house or garage or space to put the apartment contents. Our oldest son and his wife gave us a trip of a lifetime to an all-inclusive resort to Mexico in March 2017. We left two days after my husband lost his job. I was diagnosed with Primary Biliary Cirrhosis, which is a liver disease, in early March that same year.

The process of building our house was moving forward. It was a positive chaos because we were so excited, and it was a negative chaos because we wondered everyday if we would have to finish the house simply to sell our dream. Within a few short months, things started to turn around. I was offered a job working for a private firm, and my husband accepted a job in our hometown.

Our first granddaughter was born on April 20, 2017

Our daughter was expecting her second child in September 2017.

We got our occupancy permit and moved into our dream home on June 19, 2017. The planning was done for the most part. It was all working out.

And then we experienced a traumatic kind of chaos. On July 6, 2017, our youngest niece died suddenly while on her grad trip in Cuba. This would be one of the most horrible days in our lives. She was 18 years old. She had a heart attack. The process of calling our children to give them this news felt chaotic. It took moments of CALM to be able to share the news and to talk them through what information we had and doing it all over the phone was difficult. During this time, it seemed that no amount of CALM helped. Every thought, every plan, and every conversation felt chaotic, but for our children on the other end of the phone, we needed to find our CALM, if only for small amounts of time. It was a trauma for all of us.

In all the years we were raising our family, our siblings were raising their families too. We were all teaching our kids the same things and facing our own challenges. Nothing could have prepared us for the sudden death of our beloved niece. When the cousins gathered together, although a piece of them was missing, they found a CALM in sharing their memories and just by being together. The memories for these cousins were created mostly at the lake. The lake is a consistent common place for all of them.

The strength of my brother and sister-in-law has been a CALM for each of us. We don't have to work hard to honour her as she left a legacy that is unparalleled for a young girl her age. She was their baby, and she was our baby niece. She was a bright light and a beautiful soul. We have all raised great kids, and we have all had to work together to hold each other up as we work everyday to deal with this loss.

The reality of this trauma was the realization that tomorrow is not promised. For us, this was the time when we had to find our own wings. Three of our kids live in Northern Alberta. Our third child lives a five-hour drive west of our home on the lake. We didn't plan for them to be so far away, but we did hope for them to all be successful, happy, healthy, and holy people. We hoped they would know the value of friendship, and we hoped that they would always be true to their roots. We hoped that they would give back to their community and get together any chance they could. We miss them every single day, but we are so very proud of their work ethic and their commitment to their respective communities and to our family as a whole. Everyday is a gift and we have been showered with gifts.

What we have learned is the value of staying CALM, and we have learned how hard it is to do that. We have learned that some days our baggage is heavy and other days not so much. We have learned that we are all striving to raise good and happy children, and we all go about that in different ways. We have learned that losing a job, having minimal money, or having too much chaos is not the worst thing that can happen. The worst thing to experience is a death or a terminal illness. You can make more money, you can have more things, you can get another job, you can sell a house, you can change your location, you can change schools, and you can make new friends, but you can not replace a person.

Your family is yours. Embrace them. In this life there are few things that cannot be changed... your parents are your parents, your birthday is your birthday, and your siblings are your siblings. Own who you are. Understand that our parents and their parents did the best they could with what they had and what they knew. In today's world, there is more information at our fingertips, and an ever-increasing awareness of trends. Take what information you need and then set the framework for your family. It's okay to do things different than our parents, and it's okay to do things different than our parenting peers. We are all working toward the same goal. Read, learn, and ask for help. This world is moving faster than ever. I hope you can find your "Calm in the Chaos."

We all need roots and wings.

The End

EPILOGUE:

Our journey is not over. We continue to learn as parents. We continue to work through the joys and challenges of parenting our children who are adults and parents themselves.

No one can completely prepare you for this journey. There are many books, and lectures, and seminars, but the time and energy that is invested in your family is yours. There are so many differences. It has been said to me that I don't know what it's like to be a single parent or to try to make a blended family work. I have been told that I don't know what it's like to be completely disconnected from my family or to have my extended family living under the same roof. Those statements are true, but my hope is that you can be encouraged by some of the stories and events in my parenting journey and find your way. I hope you can find your CALM whenever you are feeling like you are in the midst of chaos.

We all have challenges. We are all different ages during different stages. We all have a different history. Some histories are beautiful and others traumatic. The school systems are different, the rules and laws are different now than when our parents were attending school. There are noted differences of today's school rules vs the rules that were in place even 10 years ago. As each generation changes and grows, it will be important for us to keep up with the change and grow with each new generation. We will teach them based on our past, and they will teach us as we move forward.

Embrace what you have and where you are. Embrace the changes while establishing your own way. Stand your ground and find your CALM.

Visit me on Facebook at
www.facebook.com/FINDINGCALMINTHECHAOS

Visit my website:
FindingCalmintheChaos.com

Printed in Canada